CAREER EXPLORATION

Construction Carpenter

by Rosemary Wallner

Consultant:
Associated General Contractors of America

CAPSTONE BOOKS

an imprint of Capstone Press
Mankato, Minnesota

Capstone Books are published by Capstone Press
151 Good Counsel Drive, P.O. Box 669, Mankato, Minnesota 56002
http://www.capstone-press.com

Library of Congress Cataloging-in-Publication Data
Wallner, Rosemary, 1964–
     Construction carpenter/by Rosemary Wallner.
     p. cm.—(Career exploration)
     Includes bibliographical references and index.
     Summary: Introduces the career of the construction carpenter by providing
information about educational requirements, duties, work place, salary, employment
outlook, and possible future positions.
     ISBN 0-7368-0487-0
     1. Carpentry—Vocational guidance—Juvenile literature. 2.Carpenters—
Juvenile literature. [1. Carpentry—Vocational guidance. 2. Carpenters.
3. Vocational guidance.] I. Title. II. Series.
TH5608.8.W35   2000
694'.023—dc21   99-053792

Editorial Credits

Leah K. Pockrandt, editor; Steve Christensen, cover designer; Kia Bielke, production
     designer and illustrator; Heidi Schoof, photo researcher

Photo Credits

Betty Crowell, 22, 34
Colephoto/Mark E. Gibson, 13
International Stock/Tom Carroll, 18; Keith Wood, 36; Mark Bolster, 39
Photo Network/Eric R. Berndt, 40
Robert Maust/Photo Agora, 24
Shaffer Photography/James L. Shaffer, 33
Unicorn Stock Photos/Dick Young, 6; Aneal Vohra, 9; Eric Berndt, 14; Mike
     Morris, 31
Uniphoto/Llewellyn, 10; John Neubauer, 28; David Stover, 46
Visuals Unlimited/Mark E. Gibson, 16; Jeff Greenberg, 21

2 3 4 5 6 05 04 03 02

Table of Contents

Fast Facts

Career Title	Construction Carpenter
O*NET Number	87102A
DOT Cluster (Dictionary of Occupational Titles)	Structural work
DOT Number	860.381-022
GOE Number (Guide for Occupational Exploration)	05.05.02
NOC Number (National Occupational Classification-Canada)	7271
Salary Range (U.S. Bureau of Labor Statistics and Human Resources Development Canada, late 1990s figures)	U.S.: $13,884 to $45,448 Canada: $13,700 to $50,800 (Canadian dollars)
Minimum Educational Requirements	U.S.: high school diploma Canada: high school diploma
Certification/Licensing Requirements	U.S.: none Canada: varies by province

Subject Knowledge	Design; building and construction
Personal Abilities/Skills	Skillfully use hand or power tools; read blueprints and drawings of items to be made or repaired; measure and cut materials or objects with precision; use arithmetic and shop geometry to figure amounts of materials needed, dimensions to be followed, and cost of materials; picture what finished products will look like
Job Outlook	U.S.: slower than average growth Canada: poor
Personal Interests	Mechanical: interest in applying mechanical principles to practical situations, using machines, power tools, hand tools, or techniques
Similar Types of Jobs	Bricklayers; stonemasons; electricians; plumbers; pipefitters; plasterers; concrete masons

Chapter 1

Construction Carpenter

Construction carpenters build and repair buildings and other structures. They follow drawn plans such as blueprints to construct structures.

Defining the Career

Construction carpenters work on a variety of projects. They may build houses, office buildings, and other structures. These may include wooden and steel forms for building concrete structures. Construction carpenters build walls and attach them to a structure's frame. This wooden or metal skeleton supports all the major elements of the building. Some construction carpenters also build cabinets. They attach cabinets to finished walls. This process also is called hanging cabinets.

Construction carpenters build a variety of structures.

Construction carpenters perform other tasks. They install windows and doors. They build stairs and railings. They also may lay flooring. These surfaces include tile, carpet, and vinyl or wood flooring.

Construction carpenters finish structures after they are built. They may install trim. Trim is often made of wood. Trim surrounds windows and doors inside buildings. They also may install items such as doorknobs and locks.

Construction carpenters must follow building rules. Different cities, states, and provinces have building codes that carpenters must follow. These codes make sure that all construction carpenters follow the same safety guidelines.

Work Settings

Most construction carpenters work for general contractors. These people oversee projects. Most construction carpenters work for contractors who build, remodel, or repair buildings. Some carpenters work for manufacturing firms, government agencies, schools, or retail businesses. Almost one-third of all carpenters are self-employed. They do not work full-time for one contractor or business.

Some construction carpenters install trim in buildings.

Construction carpenters work alone and in teams. They may work with other workers as part of a construction crew. Construction carpenters plan their work so that it fits into the other workers' order of tasks. For example, they build wall frames before other workers can plaster the walls. Construction carpenters also must finish some tasks before plumbers and electricians can perform their work. Plumbers

Construction carpenters must wear protective items such as a hard hat and safety glasses.

install and repair water and sewage systems such as sinks and toilets. Electricians install electrical systems and fix electrical equipment.

Hours and Conditions

Most construction carpenters work about 35 hours per week. They often work extra hours to meet project deadlines. These hours usually are on rush jobs and during busy seasons such as summer. Construction carpenters earn overtime pay for working these extra hours.

The amount of time construction carpenters work varies. Some construction carpenters work steadily all year. Others work only six to nine months per year. These carpenters may not be able to find work during slow seasons or winter months. Construction carpenters may perform small repair jobs or remodeling work during these times.

Construction carpenters often work outdoors. They work in different weather conditions. They may work on construction sites that are wet, muddy, or dusty.

Construction carpenters must follow strict safety regulations. They must wear safety glasses and a hard hat. The glasses and hat protect their eyes and head from loose particles or falling items. Some construction carpenters wear safety straps around their waist. These thick belts help carpenters avoid back injuries. Most construction carpenters wear sturdy, steel-toed work boots or shoes. These boots or shoes protect carpenters' feet.

Tools and Equipment

Construction carpenters use hand and power tools. Power tools are powered by electricity or gasoline. Most carpenters use their own tools. Some large construction businesses provide power tools for carpenters to use.

Construction carpenters use saws to cut wood and metal. They use hand saws to cut small pieces. They use power saws to cut larger pieces. They use round radial saws to cut long planks.

Construction carpenters shape wood with chisels, planes, rasps, and sanders. Carpenters use the flat, sharp ends of chisels to carve wood. Carpenters use planes to shave uneven layers off boards. Carpenters use rasps and sanders to smooth wood. Rasps are coarse files. Sanders are machines that hold sheets of sandpaper. Carpenters move sanders over wood to smooth it.

Construction carpenters use several items to join materials together. These include hammers and nails, screwdrivers and screws, and staple guns and staples. Carpenters sometimes use adhesives such as glue. They also use dowel pins. Dowel pins are round, wooden pieces that connect two pieces of wood.

Construction carpenters use other items to help them join materials. They use clamps to hold two pieces together while glue dries. They use drills and routers to cut holes into wood.

Construction carpenters must measure distances carefully and accurately.

Construction carpenters use tools for measuring. They use rulers and tape measures. They use framing squares to measure right angles.

Construction carpenters use tools to check for accuracy. They must make sure the structures are built according to blueprints. Carpenters use levels to determine if an item is straight. A level

Construction carpenters use levels to determine if boards and other surfaces are straight.

is a straight bar with an air bubble trapped in liquid. Construction carpenters hold the level against an object. The item is level if the air bubble stays in the middle of the window.

Construction carpenters use plumb lines to make sure walls are straight. A plumb line has a lead weight attached to one end of a piece of string. Construction carpenters attach the other end of the line to the top of a wall and let the lead weight drop down. They know the wall is straight if the lead weight falls straight.

Specialties

Construction carpenters must be able to perform a variety of tasks. Some construction carpenters must work on all stages of building or repair. Construction carpenters who work for large general contractors may specialize in certain areas of construction. Many of these workers are rough carpenters or finish carpenters. Rough carpenters begin construction and do duties such as set up scaffolding or build foundation frames. Finish carpenters work on buildings after rough carpenters have finished their work.

Other construction carpenters specialize in specific tasks. For example, door hangers are carpenters who specialize in hanging doors. Hardwood-floor installers specialize in installing hardwood floors in buildings.

Chapter 2

Day-to-Day Activities

Construction carpenters work on different projects. Some projects may take only a day to complete. But other projects may take many weeks or months.

Rough Carpenters

Rough carpenters begin construction projects. These carpenters build the wooden forms to hold concrete for a building foundation. They also set up scaffolding. Scaffolding consists of platforms for workers to stand on to reach high places.

Rough carpenters may build small, temporary structures. Carpenters use these structures only for a short time. Temporary structures may include small tool sheds for construction equipment. Some

Construction carpenters may work on projects that take many weeks or months to complete.

Construction carpenters review project plans with their supervisors.

rough carpenters also build field offices. Project workers use field offices for meetings and to make phone calls.

Finish Carpenters
Finish carpenters begin work on a project after rough carpenters complete their job. Finish carpenters build wood frames for walls. They also are called trim or outside carpenters.

Finish carpenters lay the subfloor. A subfloor is the base for the floor. Carpenters put down hardwood, vinyl flooring, or carpet on top of the subfloor.

Finish carpenters complete a construction job. They install paneling on the walls. They put up ceiling tiles. They hang kitchen cabinets. They put in doors and windows. They install window locks, door locks, and door handles.

Starting a Project

Construction carpenters begin each project by meeting with supervisors. Supervisors oversee the work of others. Supervisors explain the project to the carpenters.

Construction carpenters review the project blueprints with the supervisors. Blueprints include the building's dimensions and materials needed. Dimensions are a building's measurements.

Rough carpenters build the forms for the foundation. They use levels and framing squares to measure each corner and side of the form. Other workers pour the concrete when the rough carpenters are finished.

Building and Finishing a Project

Rough carpenters begin building a structure's framework after the concrete foundation is dry. They set anchor bolts in the foundation to attach the framework. They set up floor joists and subfloors. Joists are beams that support the subfloor of a building. Rough carpenters set up the pre-built trusses. Trusses are brackets that support the roof. Rough carpenters also make cuts through floors and walls for pipes or wires to pass through.

Finish carpenters have more jobs after the framework is up. They install frames for the windows and doors. Some finish carpenters put insulation and fireproofing materials between the framework. They nail wood or metal strips to studs to guide plasterers or drywall installers. They then fit and nail a special covering over the framework. This makes the outside walls and the roof of the structure.

Finish carpenters have other jobs after the walls and roof are in place. For example, they

Rough carpenters construct the framework for a building.

lay the floors. They also put paneling on walls and install ceiling tiles.

Finish carpenters install many items. They also put in windows and put up inside and outside trim. Finish carpenters also hang cabinets and doors.

Chapter 3

The Right Candidate

Construction carpenters need a variety of skills and abilities. They must solve math problems. They must be able to work with different types of tools and materials. Carpenters must work well with others. They also must be able to follow instructions.

Skills and Abilities

Construction carpenters need a basic knowledge of building design. They must know the qualities of the different woods and materials they use. They must know the basic procedures and standards of other workers in the building trade.

Construction carpenters need math skills. These skills help them measure a building's dimensions. Construction carpenters use math

Construction carpenters must work well with others.

Construction carpenters need to be able to communicate with other carpenters and workers.

to figure out the amount of materials they need for a job. They may use math to figure how much materials cost. Construction carpenters must be able to solve these math problems quickly and accurately. Carpenters also must measure and cut materials accurately.

Construction carpenters must be able to work in different conditions. They should be able to work in tight spaces or high places. They may have to work below a stairway or on a roof. Construction carpenters need good balance. They must be able to keep their balance when working on scaffolding or roofs.

Construction carpenters must work well with others. They often work with other carpenters and workers to complete projects. They must be able to work with different types of people.

Construction carpenters need good communication skills. They must discuss building plans with supervisors and other workers. They must listen well. They need to understand specific instructions.

Construction carpenters should be able to imagine what finished products will look like. This helps construction carpenters lay out floors and erect walls correctly.

Skills

Workplace Skills

Yes / No

Resources:
- Assign use of time ☑ ☐
- Assign use of money ☑ ☐
- Assign use of material and facility resources ☑ ☐
- Assign use of human resources ☑ ☐

Interpersonal Skills:
- Take part as a member of a team ☑ ☐
- Teach others ☑ ☐
- Serve clients/customers ☑ ☐
- Show leadership ☑ ☐
- Work with others to arrive at a decision ☑ ☐
- Work with a variety of people ☑ ☐

Information:
- Acquire and judge information ☑ ☐
- Understand and follow legal requirements ☑ ☐
- Organize and maintain information ☑ ☐
- Understand and communicate information ☑ ☐
- Use computers to process information ☑ ☐

Systems:
- Identify, understand, and work with systems ☑ ☐
- Understand environmental, social, political, economic, or business systems ☑ ☐
- Oversee and correct system performance ☐ ☑
- Improve and create systems ☐ ☑

Technology:
- Select technology ☑ ☐
- Apply technology to task ☑ ☐
- Maintain and troubleshoot technology ☑ ☐

Foundation Skills

Basic Skills:
- Read ☑ ☐
- Write ☑ ☐
- Do arithmetic and math ☑ ☐
- Speak and listen ☑ ☐

Thinking Skills:
- Learn ☑ ☐
- Reason ☑ ☐
- Think creatively ☑ ☐
- Make decisions ☑ ☐
- Solve problems ☑ ☐

Personal Qualities:
- Take individual responsibility ☑ ☐
- Have self-esteem and self-management ☑ ☐
- Be sociable ☑ ☐
- Be fair, honest, and sincere ☑ ☐

Physical Condition

Construction carpenters should be in good health. Their work is strenuous. The job requires a great deal of physical labor. Carpenters often stand for long periods of time. They also must climb, bend, and kneel while they work.

Construction carpenters must be careful. Falling objects may injure them. They risk injury from slips or falls. They also risk injury from working with sharp or rough materials. They must be careful when using sharp tools and power equipment. Carpenters need good hand-eye coordination to prevent injury from these tools.

Chapter 4

Preparing for the Career

Most people who want to become construction carpenters begin their training after high school. Most people become apprentices. They spend several years learning the trade. Some people begin their training in high school. They take carpentry and vocational education classes.

High School Education

People who want to become construction carpenters should take a variety of classes in high school. Students should take vocational education classes and mechanical drafting or drawing classes. Students learn how objects are constructed in vocational education classes such as shop or carpentry. They also get

---

People who want to be construction carpenters may take training classes or become apprentices.

experience working with tools in machine shop classes. Students learn how to draw blueprints in mechanical drafting or drawing classes.

Math and physics classes are useful to students. Students learn how to solve complex math problems in math classes. They learn how heat, light, sound, and electricity work in physics classes.

Some high school students take basic mechanics courses. These students work with general contractors. They learn about the tools construction carpenters use and how buildings are constructed. These programs usually last two to three years.

High school students also may gain experience outside of school. Students may work part-time or during the summer as carpenter's helpers. These students work for contractors or self-employed carpenters. Students learn basic carpentry skills at these jobs.

Most employers prefer to hire high school graduates. People who want to become carpenters may learn on the job or complete training programs. These formal training programs are called apprenticeship programs. Apprentices learn carpentry skills by working with skilled people and attending classes.

High school students may gain carpentry experience in shop or carpentry classes.

Apprenticeship Programs

Apprenticeship training is one of the most common ways to acquire the skills needed in the construction trades. Most apprentices are high school graduates who are at least 18 years old. Some apprentices also may have attended vocational or technical schools. Apprentices must be in good physical condition.

Apprentice programs are available throughout the United States and Canada. The programs usually take three to four years to complete. The length of a program depends on an apprentice's skills.

Professional organizations offer apprenticeship programs. The Associated Builders and Contractors Trade Association and the United Brotherhood of Carpenters and Joiners of America offer apprenticeship programs. Chapters of the Associated General Contractors of America and the National Association of Home Builders also offer apprenticeship programs.

Apprenticeship programs combine on-the-job training with classroom instruction. Apprentices perform about 8,000 hours of on-the-job training. During their training, apprentices learn to safely use and care for construction tools and equipment. They learn basic structural design. They also learn to perform tasks such as form building, rough framing, and finishing.

Apprentices must complete about 570 hours of classroom work. They learn blueprint reading, safety procedures, and first aid. They also review basic math skills.

Most apprentices earn wages for the hours they work. Their wages increase as they learn more.

Apprentices receive on-the-job training and classroom instruction.

Starting pay for apprentices begins at about half of a journeyman's rate. A journeyman is a person who has completed apprenticeship. This person should earn the highest minimum wage rate for the job. At the end of the program, apprentices earn the same salary as journeyman carpenters.

Informal Training
Many people learn construction skills through informal on-the-job training. These people learn by

Large general contractors may provide training in several carpentry areas.

working with skilled carpenters. But some acquire skills by attending vocational or trade schools.

On-the-job training usually is less thorough than an apprenticeship. The amount of training and supervision depends on the size of the construction company. A small contractor that specializes in building homes may only provide training in rough framing. But a large general contractor may provide training in several carpentry tasks.

Certification

Construction carpenters in the United States can work after they complete an apprenticeship program or have on-the-job training. They do not need to be certified to work.

Construction carpenters in Canada may benefit from being trade certified. Some employers prefer to hire certified carpenters. Employers know that certified construction carpenters have a full understanding of the profession. In Quebec, carpenters must be certified.

To gain trade certification, carpenters must complete an apprenticeship program. This program may take three to four years to complete. Construction carpenters also may gain certification by having more than four years' experience. These carpenters also must have taken some carpentry classes in high school or trade school.

Some carpenters in Canada may obtain interprovincial trade certification. These carpenters earn a certificate called the Red Seal. With this certificate, carpenters can work in provinces throughout Canada.

Chapter 5

The Market

Construction carpenters have many job opportunities. As they gain experience, they may advance to better positions and earn higher salaries.

Salary

Construction carpenters' salaries vary in the United States and Canada. In the United States, most carpenters earn between $13,884 and $45,448 per year. The average salary for carpenters in the United States is about $24,752 per year.

In Canada, most construction carpenters earn between $13,700 and $50,800 per year. The average salary for construction carpenters is about $32,500 per year.

Construction carpenters' salaries depend on many factors. These include skills, duties, and job

Construction carpenters' job opportunities may increase as they gain experience.

locations. Construction carpenters may earn more in certain areas such as large cities. Construction carpenters also may earn less at certain times during the year. For example, some carpenters may not be able to work during cold or rainy weather.

Construction carpenters with special skills often earn more money than general carpenters. For example, finish carpenters who specialize in installing hardwood floors may earn more money. Crew leaders also receive higher wages than the workers on their crews. Crew leaders oversee the work of other carpenters.

Job Outlook

Carpentry is the largest construction trade. Many job opportunities are available for carpenters.

In the United States, carpenters face a varied job outlook. Thousands of job openings will become available each year as construction carpenters leave the field. Some people leave the field because they dislike the work or cannot find steady employment. This creates many job openings.

The job outlook is affected by the demand for new housing and business buildings. An increased demand for carpenters creates

There are many job opportunities for construction carpenters in the United States.

additional job openings. But employment is expected to have slower than average growth. Additional construction may not always create new jobs.

In Canada, the job outlook is poor. Not enough jobs exist for the number of new construction carpenters entering the field. But the job outlook varies across the country. Carpenters may have more job opportunities in areas where many companies are located.

Some experienced construction carpenters start their own construction businesses.

Advancement Opportunities

Construction carpenters may advance as they gain experience. Some construction carpenters advance to carpentry supervisors or general construction supervisors. These carpenters know about the entire construction process. They estimate the types and amounts of materials needed for a project. They estimate a project's cost. They also estimate how long a project will take to complete.

Some experienced carpenters start their own construction businesses. These construction carpenters are called independent contractors. These carpenters meet with clients, hire carpentry crews, and purchase supplies.

Related Occupations

People interested in construction have many job opportunities in the building trades. They may become bricklayers, electricians, plumbers, or plasterers. These people often work with construction carpenters. They specialize in specific areas of construction.

Construction carpenters have opportunities in a variety of industries. They are needed to build business buildings, factories, and homes. They also are needed to remodel and repair structures. Their skills are necessary to fill many construction needs.

Words to Know

apprentice (uh-PREN-tiss)—someone who learns a trade or craft by working with a skilled worker

blueprint (BLOO-print)—a detailed plan for a building or other structure

dimension (duh-MEN-shuhn)—an object's measurement or its size; an object's dimensions are length, width, and height.

electrician (i-lek-TRISH-uhn)—someone who installs electrical systems and fixes electrical equipment

foundation (foun-DAY-shuhn)—a solid base on which a structure is built; structures include buildings and bridges.

plumber (PLUHM-ur)—someone who puts in and repairs water and sewage systems including pipes, sinks, and toilets

scaffolding (SKAF-uhld-ing)—a structure made of wooden planks and ropes or metal poles; workers stand on scaffolds when they work above the ground on a building or other structure.

stud (STUHD)—a small upright piece of wood in the framing of the walls of a building; drywall, paneling, or boards are attached to studs.

subfloor (SUHB-flor)—the base for a floor of a building

To Learn More

Construction: Career in Focus. Chicago: Ferguson Publishing, 1999.

Cosgrove, Holli, ed. *Career Discovery Encyclopedia.* Vol. 2. Chicago: Ferguson Publishing, 2000.

Sheldon, Roger. *Opportunities in Carpentry Careers.* VGM Opportunities. Lincolnwood, Ill.: VGM Career Horizons, 1999.

Sumichrast, Michael. *Opportunities in Building Construction Trades.* VGM Opportunities. Lincolnwood, Ill.: VGM Career Horizons, 1999.

Young Person's Occupational Outlook Handbook. Indianapolis: JIST Works, 1999.

Useful Addresses

Associated General Contractors of America
333 John Carlyle Street
Suite 200
Alexandria, VA 22314

Canadian Construction Association
75 Albert Street
Suite 400
Ottawa, ON K1P 5E7
Canada

**United Brotherhood of Carpenters and
 Joiners of America**
101 Constitution Avenue NW
Washington, DC 20001

Internet Sites

Associated General Contractors of America
http://www.agc.org

Canadian Construction Association
http://www.cca-acc.com

Job Futures—Carpenters
http://www.jobfutures.ca/jobfutures/
   noc/7271.html

**Occupational Outlook Handbook—
   Carpenters**
http://stats.bls.gov/oco/ocos202.htm

Index